CW00394603

Tell everyone
Now, today, I shall
sing beautifully for
my friends' pleasure.

Mary Barnard (b. 1909)

Τάδε νῦν ἐταίραις
ταῖς ἔμαισι τέρπνα κάλως ἀείσω.

Sappho, *fragment*

A GARDEN *of* GREEK VERSE

POEMS OF ANCIENT GREECE

F

FRANCES LINCOLN LIMITED
PUBLISHERS

CONTENTS

WHAT A PIECE OF WORK IS A MAN!

Wonders are many, but there is no wonder
Wilder than Man –
Man who makes the winds of winter bear him,
Through the trough of waves that tower about him,
Across grey wastes of sea;
Man who wearies the untiring, the immortal –
Earth, eldest of the gods, as year by year,
His plough-teams come and go.
The care-free bands of birds,
Beasts of the wild, tribes of the sea,
In netted toils he takes,
The Subtle One.

Frank Laurence Lucas (1894–1967)

Πολλὰ τὰ δεινὰ κοὐδὲν ἀν-
θρώπου δεινότερον πέλει·
τοῦτο καὶ πολιοῦ πέραν
πόντου χειμερίῳ νότῳ
χωρεῖ, περιβρυχίοισιν
περῶν ὑπ᾽ οἴδμασιν, θεῶν
τε τὰν ὑπερτάταν, Γᾶν
ἄφθιτον, ἀκαμάταν ἀποτρύεται,
ἰλλομένων ἀρότρων ἔτος εἰς ἔτος,
ἱππείῳ γένει πολεύων.

κουφονόων τε φῦλον ὀρ-
νίθων ἀμφιβαλὼν ἀγρεῖ
καὶ θηρῶν ἀγρίων ἔθνη
πόντου τ᾽ εἰναλίαν φύσιν
σπείραισι δικτυοκλώστοις,
περιφραδὴς ἀνήρ.

Sophocles, *Antigone*

ATHENA ARMS HERSELF FOR WAR

Now heaven's dread arms her mighty limbs invest,
Jove's cuirass blazes on her ample breast;
Decked in sad triumph for the mournful field,
O'er her broad shoulders hangs his horrid shield,
Dire, black, tremendous! Round the margin rolled
A fringe of serpents hissing guards the gold:
Here all the terrors of grim war appear,
Here rages Force, here tremble Flight and Fear,
Here stormed Contention, and here Fury frowned,
And the dire orb portentous Gorgon crowned.

Alexander Pope (1688–1744)

Αὐτὰρ Ἀθηναίη, κούρη Διὸς αἰγιόχοιο,
πέπλον μὲν κατέχευεν ἑανὸν πατρὸς ἐπ' οὔδει,
ποικίλον, ὅν ῥ' αὐτὴ ποιήσατο καὶ κάμε χερσίν·
ἡ δὲ χιτῶν' ἐνδῦσα Διὸς νεφεληγερέταο
τεύχεσιν ἐς πόλεμον θωρήσσετο δακρυόεντα.
ἀμφὶ δ' ἄρ' ὤμοισιν βάλετ' αἰγίδα θυσσανόεσσαν
δεινήν, ἣν περὶ μὲν πάντῃ Φόβος ἐστεφάνωται,
ἐν δ' Ἔρις, ἐν δ' Ἀλκή, ἐν δὲ κρυόεσσα Ἰωκή,
ἐν δέ τε Γοργείη κεφαλὴ δεινοῖο πελώρου,
δεινή τε σμερδνή τε, Διὸς τέρας αἰγιόχοιο.

Homer, *Iliad V*

BRIEF LIFE

See, how our lives like birds take wing,
Like sparks that fly when a fire soars,
To the shore of the god of evening.

Dudley Fitts (1903–68) and
Robert Fitzgerald (1902–87)

Ἄλλον δ' ἂν ἄλλῳ προσίδοις ἅπερ εὔπτερον ὄρνιν
κρεῖσσον ἀμαιμακέτου πυρὸς ὄρμενον
ἀκτὰν πρὸς ἑσπέρου θεοῦ.

Sophocles, *Oedipus the King*

A TRIAL OF LOVE

Water bring, and bring me wine,
Bring the wreaths where flowers entwine;
Hasten, lad; our fists we try,
Matched together, love and I.

Thomas Farrant Higham (1890–1975)

Φέρ᾽ ὕδωρ, φέρ᾽ οἶνον, ὦ παῖ, φέρε δ᾽ ἀνθεμόεντας ἡμὶν
στεφάνους ἔνεικον, ὡς δὴ πρὸς Ἔρωτα πυκταλίζω.

Anacreon, *fragment*

WORSHIP

Sweet child, with garlands be thy tresses bound,
Twine marjoram with woodbine, spray with spray;
The gods love those who come with chaplets crowned,
From those ungarlanded they turn away.

A.C. Benson (1862–1925)

Σὺ δὲ στεφάνοις, ὦ Δίκα, πέρθεσθ' ἐράτοις φόβαισιν
ὄρπακας ἀνήτω συναέρραισ' ἀπάλαισι χέρσιν·
εὐάνθεα γὰρ πέλεται καὶ Χάριτες μάκαιραι
μᾶλλον ποτόρην, ἀστεφανώτοισι δ' ἀπυστρέφονται.

Sappho, *fragment*

A DIVINE TRUTH

Whom the gods love die young.

Lord Byron (1788–1824)

Ὃν οἱ θεοὶ φιλοῦσιν ἀποθνήσκει νέος.

Menander, *fragment*

WEEP FOR YOUTH'S PASSING

What fools men are to weep the dead and gone!
Unwept, youth drops its petals one by one.

Thomas Farrant Higham (1890–1975)

Ἄφρονες ἄνθρωποι καὶ νήπιοι, οἵτε θανόντας
κλαίουσ', οὐδ' ἥβης ἄνθος ἀπολλύμενον.

Theognis, *Elegies*

LOVE'S ANGUISH

Mother, I cannot mind my wheel;
  My fingers ache, my lips are dry:
Oh! if you felt the pain I feel!
  But oh, whoever felt as I?

No longer could I doubt him true;
  All other men may use deceit:
He always said my eyes were blue,
  And often swore my lips were sweet.

Walter Savage Landor (1775–1864)

Γλύκηα μᾶτερ, οὔτοι δύναμαι κρέκην τὸν ἴστον
πόθῳ δάμεισα παῖδος βραδίναν δι' Ἀφροδίταν.

Sappho, *fragment*

ALL THE WORLD'S A STAGE

This life a theatre we well may call,
Where every actor must perform with art;
Or laugh it through and make a farce of all,
Or learn to bear with grace his tragic part.

Robert Bland (1779–1825)

Σκηνὴ πᾶς ὁ βίος καὶ παίγνιον· ἢ μάθε παίζειν,
τὴν σπουδὴν μεταθείς, ἢ φέρε τὰς ὀδύνας.

Palladas, *Greek Anthology X*

THE POWER OF LOVE

My children, know love is not love alone,
But in her name lie many names concealed:
For she is death, imperishable force,
Desire unmixed, wild frenzy, lamentation;
In her are summed all impulses that drive
To violence, energy, tranquillity.
Deep in each living breast the goddess sinks,
And all become her prey; the tribes that swim,
The fourfoot tribes that pace upon the earth,
Harbour her; and in birds her wing is sovereign,
In beasts, in mortal men, in gods above.

Sir Richard Livingstone (1880–1960)

Ὦ παῖδες, ἥ τοι Κύπρις οὐ Κύπρις μόνον,
ἀλλ᾽ ἐστὶ πολλῶν ὀνομάτων ἐπώνυμος.
ἔστιν μὲν Ἅιδης, ἔστι δ᾽ ἄφθιτος βία,
ἔστιν δὲ λύσσα μανίας, ἔστι δ᾽ ἵμερος
ἄκρατος, ἔστ᾽ οἰμωγμός. ἐν κείνῃ τὸ πᾶν
σπουδαῖον, ἡσυχαῖον, εἰς βίαν ἄγον.
ἐντήκεται γὰρ πλευμόνων ὅσοις ἔνι
ψυχή· τίς οὐχὶ τῆσδε δεύτερος θεοῦ;
εἰσέρχεται μὲν ἰχθύων πλωτῷ γένει,
χέρσου δ᾽ ἔνεστιν ἐν τετρασκελεῖ γονῇ·
νωμᾷ δ᾽ ἐν οἰωνοῖσι τοὐκείνης πτερόν,
ἐν θηρσίν, ἐν βροτοῖσιν, ἐν θεοῖς ἄνω.

Sophocles, *fragment*

HALF-GOD

I am a god of low estate,
  Of little boons and humble things;
And if thou seek for nothing great,
  Meet recompense the morrow brings.

Whate'er a son of toil may claim,
  And my humility afford,
I grant it: – never ask my name;
  Of little things I am the lord.

A.C. Benson (1862–1925)

Κἀμὲ τὸν ἐν σμικροῖς ὀλίγον θεὸν ἢν ἐπιβώσῃς
εὐκαίρως, τεύξῃ· μὴ μεγάλων δὲ γλίχου.
ὡς ὅ τι δημοτέρων δύναται θεὸς ἀνδρὶ πενέστῃ
δωρεῖσθαι, τούτων κύριός εἰμι Τύχων.

Perses, *Greek Anthology IX*

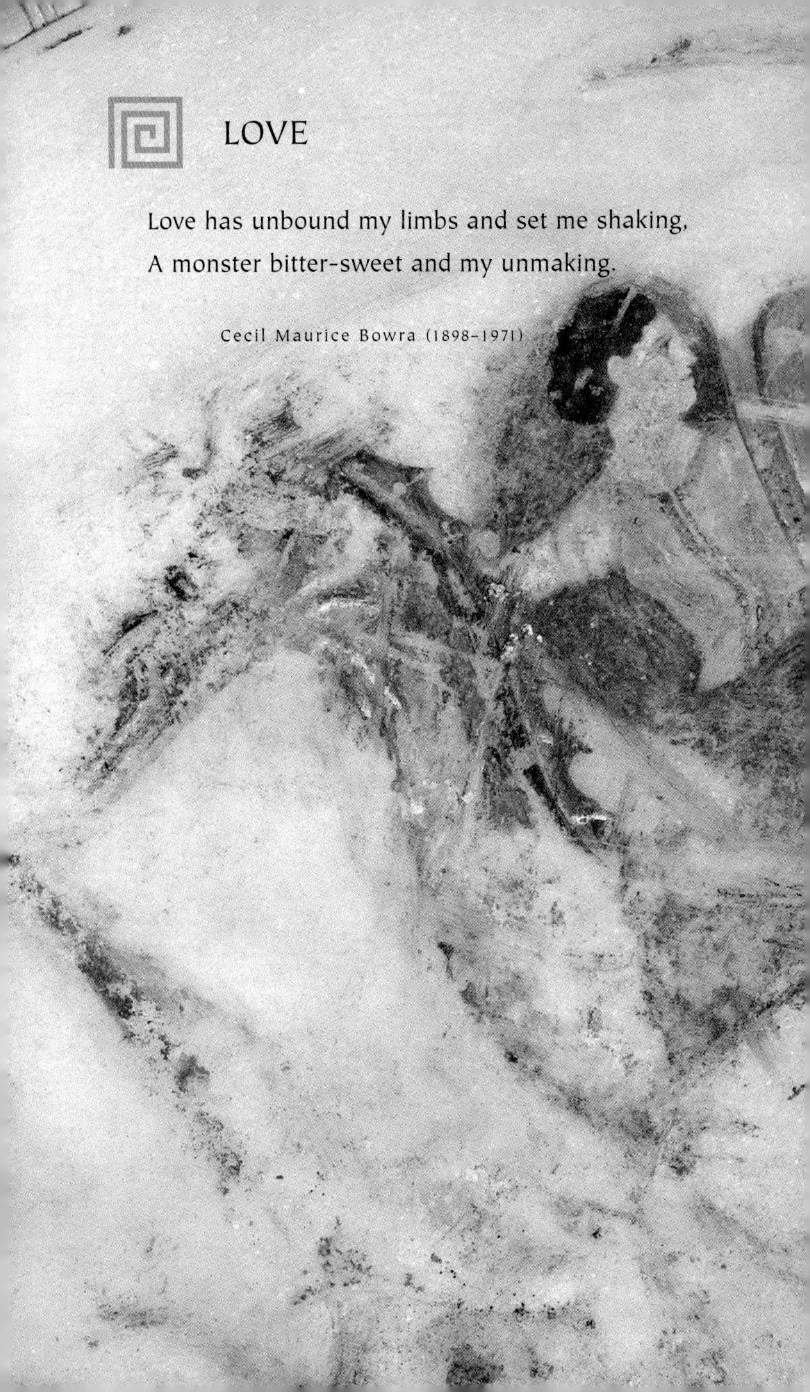

LOVE

Love has unbound my limbs and set me shaking,
A monster bitter-sweet and my unmaking.

Cecil Maurice Bowra (1898–1971)

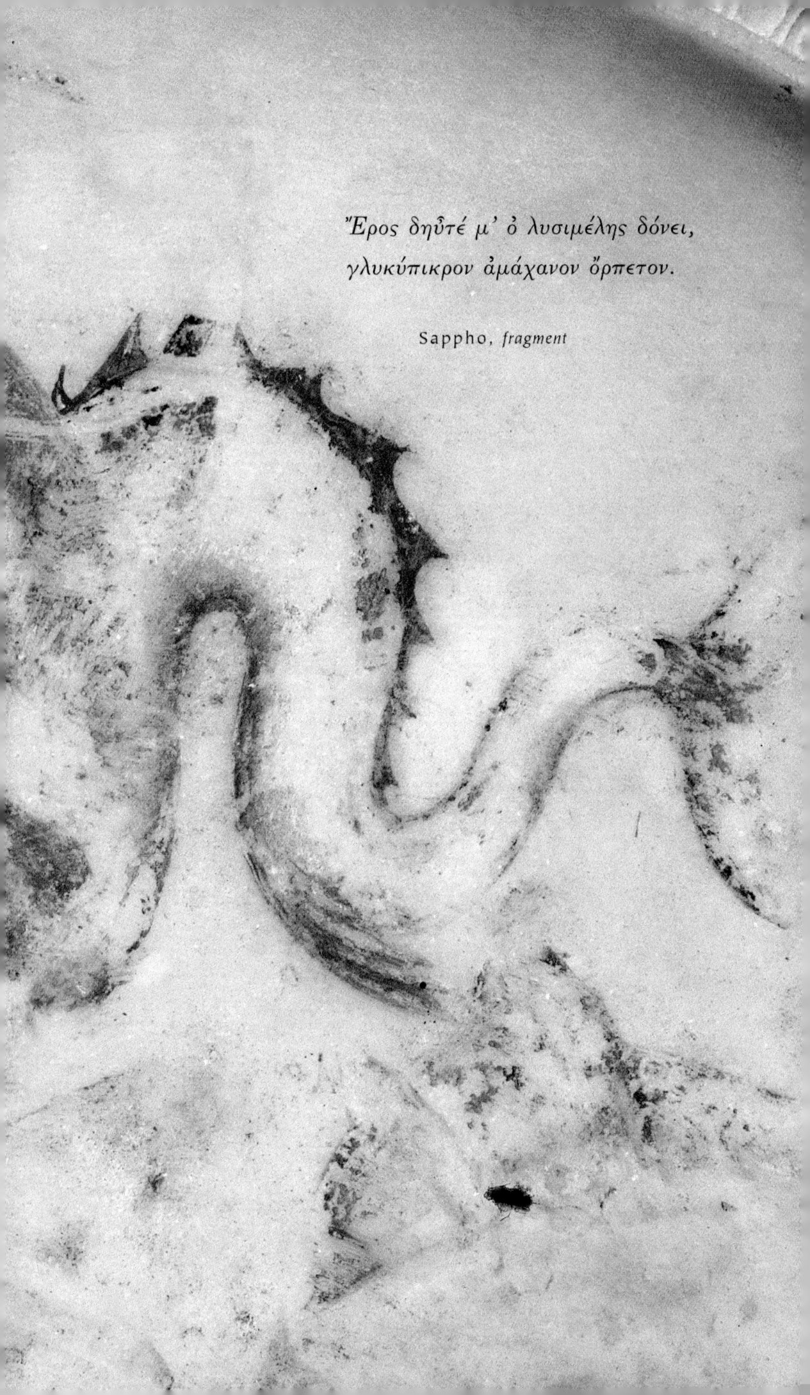

Ἔρος δηὖτέ μ’ ὀ λυσιμέλης δόνει,
γλυκύπικρον ἀμάχανον ὄρπετον.

Sappho, *fragment*

THE POWER OF THE GOD

Distinguish god in your imaginings
From men that die, think not of him as flesh.
You know him not. Sometimes he leaps in fire,
Swift, unapproachable; sometimes in water
Comes, or in the darkness clothed about,
And still is god in likeness of a beast,
In wind, cloud, lightning, thunder and rain.
The sea and all the rocks therein obey him;
Springs, rivers, tributaries all are his.
The mountains tremble, earth and
    the nethermost depths
Of monstrous ocean, earth and
    the mountain-tops
Tremble before the terrible eye of god,
A lord most powerful, in praise most high.

Thomas Farrant Higham (1890–1975)

Χώριζε θνητῶν τὸν θεὸν καὶ μὴ δόκει
ὅμοιον αὐτοῖς σάρκινον καθεστάναι.
οὐκ οἶσθα δ' αὐτόν· ποτὲ μὲν ὡς πῦρ φαίνεται
ἄπλατος ὁρμῇ, ποτὲ δ' ὕδωρ, ποτὲ γνόφος·
καὶ θηρσὶν αὐτὸς γίνεται παρεμφερής,
ἀνέμῳ νεφέλῃ τε, κἀστραπῇ βροντῇ βροχῇ,
ὑπηρετεῖ δ' αὐτῷ θάλασσα καὶ πέτραι
καὶ πᾶσα πηγὴ χὔδατος συστήματα·
τρέμει δ' ὄρη καὶ γαῖα καὶ πελώριος
βυθὸς θαλάσσης κὠρέων ὕψος μέγα,
ὅταν ἐπιβλέψῃ γοργὸν ὄμμα δεσπότου.
πάντα δύναται γάρ· δόξα δ' ὑψίστου θεοῦ.

Anonymous

THE SHIELD

I am Alexander's shield,
Borne by him on many a field;
Phoebus of the golden hair
Hath me now, an offering rare.

I am dinted, old, and dim;
Worn my boss and worn my rim;
But to eyes that see, I shine
With thy valour, master mine.

When his arm I did enfold,
I was bold, for he was bold,
Never was I known to yield,
I am Alexander's shield.

A.C. Benson (1862–1925)

Ἀσπὶς Ἀλεξάνδρου τοῦ Φυλλέος ἱερὸν ἅδε
δῶρον Ἀπόλλωνι χρυσοκόμῳ δέδομαι,
γηραλέα μὲν ἴτυν πολέμων ὕπο, γηραλέα δὲ
ὀμφαλόν· ἀλλ' ἀρετᾷ λάμπομαι, ἃν ἔκιχον
ἀνδρὶ κορυσσαμένα σὺν ἀριστέϊ, ὅς μ' ἀνέθηκε.
ἐμμὶ δ' ἀήσσατος πάμπαν ἀφ' οὗ γενόμαν.

Mnasalcas, *Greek Anthology VI*

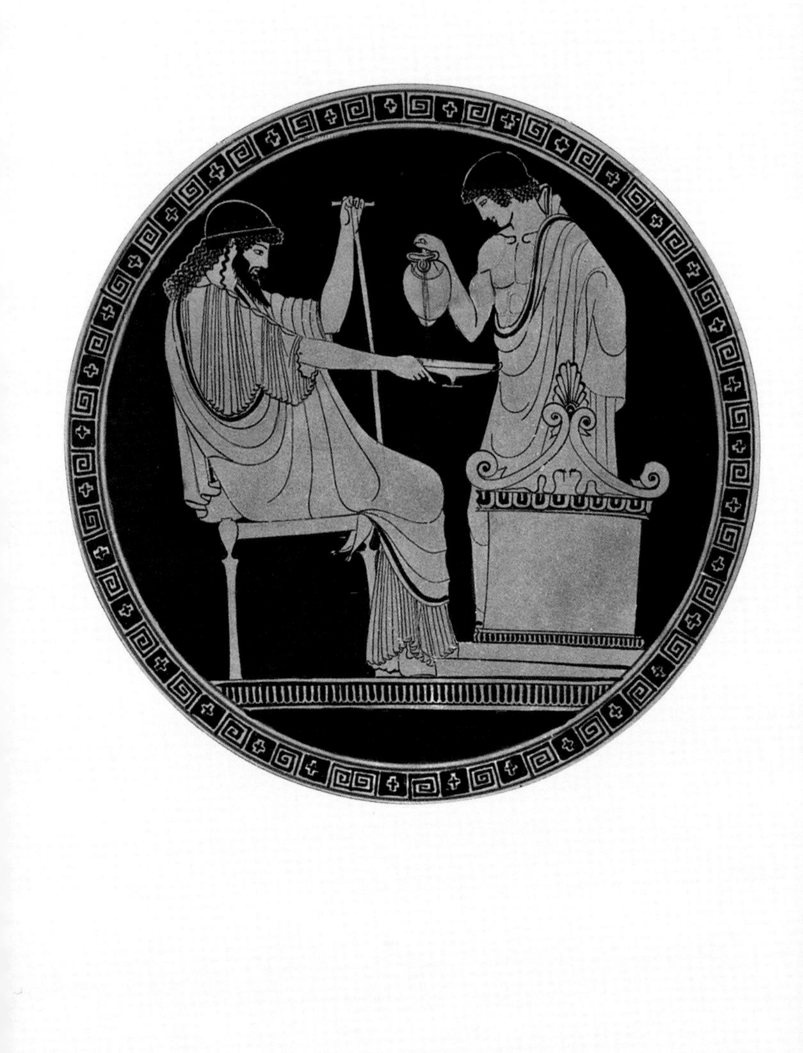

A VERY ANCIENT PROVERB

There's many a slip
'tween the cup and the lip.

David Macbeth Moir (1798–1851)

Πολλὰ μεταξὺ πέλει κύλικος καὶ χείλεος ἄκρου.

Anonymous

QUID SIT FUTURUM

Drink and be merry: there is no man knows
Tomorrow, or thereafter, how it goes:
Run not nor strive;
Give, share, and eat; be kindly as you can;
Think only thoughts that do befit a man;
Dead or alive,
Between the two's not much to choose:
Life is just that, a dip of weighing-pans;
Quick, and you take the lot,
But if you die, 'tis all another man's,
And you have not.

Sir William Sinclair Marris (1873–1945)

Πῖνε καὶ εὐφραίνου· τί γὰρ αὔριον, ἢ τί τὸ μέλλον,
οὐδεὶς γινώσκει. μὴ τρέχε, μὴ κοπία,
ὡς δύνασαι, χάρισαι, μετάδος, φάγε, θνητὰ λογίζου·
τὸ ζῆν τοῦ μὴ ζῆν οὐδὲν ὅλως ἀπέχει.
πᾶς ὁ βίος τοιόσδε, ῥοπὴ μόνον· ἂν προλάβῃς, σοῦ,
ἂν δὲ θάνῃς, ἑτέρου πάντα, σὺ δ᾽ οὐδὲν ἔχεις.

Anonymous

REMEMBRANCE OF THINGS PAST

They told me, Heraclitus, they told me you were dead;
They brought me bitter news to hear and bitter tears to shed.
I wept, as I remembered, how often you and I
Had tired the sun with talking and sent him down the sky.

And now that thou art lying, my dear old Carian guest,
A handful of grey ashes, long, long ago at rest,
Still are thy pleasant voices, thy nightingales, awake,
For Death, he taketh all away, but them he cannot take.

William Cory (1823–92)

Εἶπέ τις Ἡράκλειτε τεὸν μόρον, ἐς δέ με δάκρυ
ἤγαγεν, ἐμνήσθην δ' ὁσσάκις ἀμφότεροι
ἥλιον ἐν λέσχῃ κατεδύσαμεν· ἀλλὰ σὺ μέν που
ξεῖν' Ἁλικαρνησεῦ τετράπαλαι σποδιή·
αἱ δὲ τεαὶ ζώουσιν ἀηδόνες, ᾗσιν ὁ πάντων
ἁρπακτὴς Ἀίδης οὐκ ἐπὶ χεῖρα βαλεῖ.

Callimachus, *Epigrams II*

THE OLD MEN

Alas, how right the ancient saying is:
We, who are old, are nothing else but noise
And shape. Like mimicries of dreams we go,
And have no wits, although we think us wise.

Cecil Maurice Bowra (1898–1971)

Φεῦ φεῦ, παλαιὸς αἶνος ὡς καλῶς ἔχει·
γέροντες οὐδέν ἐσμεν ἄλλο πλὴν ψόφος
καὶ σχῆμ᾽, ὀνείρων δ᾽ ἕρπομεν μιμήματα·
νοῦς δ᾽ οὐκ ἔνεστιν, οἰόμεσθα δ᾽ εὖ φρονεῖν.

Euripides, *Aeolus, fragment*

HYMEN HYMENAON!

Hymen Hymenaon!

Raise the rafters! Hoist
them higher! Here comes
a bridegroom taller
than Ares!

Hymen Hymenaon!

He towers
above tall men as
poets of Lesbos
over all others!

Sing Hymen
O Hymenaon.

Mary Barnard (b. 1909)

Ἴψοι δὴ τὸ μέλαθρον,
ὑμήναον,
ἀέρρετε, τέκτονες ἄνδρες·
ὑμήναον.
γάμβρος εἰσέρχεται ἶσος Ἄρευι,
ἄνδρος μεγάλω πόλυ μέσδων.

Sappho, *fragment*

DIONYSUS IS STOLEN AWAY ON A SHIP

The sailors, under arms, observe their prize,
When lo, strange doings interrupt their eyes;
For first, a fountain of sweet-smelling wine
Came gushing o'er the deck with sprightly shine;
And odours, not of earth, their senses took;
The pallid wonder spread from look to look;
And then a vine-tree overran the sail,
Its green arms tossing to the pranksome gale;
And then an ivy, with a flowering shoot,
Ran up the mast in rings, and kissed the fruit,
Which here and there the dipping vine let down;
On every oar there was a garland crown.

. . . .

But now, in his own shape, the god's at hand,
And spurning first the Captain from the side,
The rest leaped after in the plunging tide;
For one and all, as they had done the same,
The same deserved; and dolphins they became.

Leigh Hunt (1784–1859)

Ἀμφὶ δ᾽ ἄρ᾽ ὅπλα
καττάνυσαν· τάχα δέ σφιν ἐφαίνετο θαυματὰ ἔργα.
οἶνος μὲν πρώτιστα θοὴν ἀνὰ νῆα μέλαιναν
ἡδύποτος κελάρυζ᾽ εὐώδης, ὤρνυτο δ᾽ ὀδμὴ
ἀμβροσίη· ναύτας δὲ τάφος λάβε πάντας ἰδόντας.
αὐτίκα δ᾽ ἀκρότατον παρὰ ἱστίον ἐξετανύσθη
ἄμπελος ἔνθα καὶ ἔνθα, κατεκρημνῶντο δὲ πολλοὶ
βότρυες· ἀμφ᾽ ἱστὸν δὲ μέλας εἱλίσσετο κισσὸς
ἄνθεσι τηλεθάων, χαρίεις δ᾽ ἐπὶ καρπὸς ὀρώρει·
πάντες δὲ σκαλμοὶ στεφάνους ἔχον·

ὁ δ᾽ ἐξαπίνης ἐπορούσας
ἀρχὸν ἕλ᾽, οἱ δὲ θύραζε κακὸν μόρον ἐξαλύοντες
πάντες ὁμῶς πήδησαν ἐπεὶ ἴδον εἰς ἅλα δῖαν,
δελφῖνες δ᾽ ἐγένοντο.

Homeric Hymns VII

POSEIDON'S COURTIERS

Round thee sport in joyous rout
  Lightly leaping, gleaming, glancing,
  Tossing in their finny dancing
Bristly mane and flattened snout,
Dolphins, whom the Muse enthrals –
  Playmates 'neath the briny waters
  Chasing Amphitrite's daughters
  In the Nereids' halls.

Herbert Kynaston (1835–1910)

Βραγχίοις περὶ δὲ σὲ πλωτοὶ
θῆρες χορεύουσι κύκλῳ,
κούφοισι ποδῶν ῥίμμασιν
ἐλάφρ᾽ ἀναπαλλόμενοι, σιμοί,
φριξαύχενες, ὠκύδρομοι σκύλακες, φιλόμουσοι
δελφῖνες, ἔναλα θρέμματα
κουρᾶν Νηρεΐδων θεᾶν,
ἃς ἐγείνατ᾽ Ἀμφιτρίτα.

Arion *(attributed)*

REALIZATION

Now I know why Eros,
Of all the progeny of
Earth and Heaven, has
been most dearly loved.

Mary Barnard (b. 1909)

Φίλτατον Γαίας γένος Ὀρράνω τε.

Sappho, *fragment*

TO HIS LYRE

I wish to tune my quivering lyre,
To deeds of fame, and notes of fire;
To echo from its rising swell,
How heroes fought, and nations fell;
When Atreus' sons advanced to war,
Or Tyrian Cadmus roved afar;
But still, to martial strains unknown,
My lyre recurs to love alone.

Lord Byron (1788–1824)

Θέλω λέγειν Ἀτρείδας,
θέλω δὲ Κάδμον ᾄδειν,
ἁ βάρβιτος δὲ χορδαῖς
Ἔρωτα μοῦνον ἠχεῖ.
ἤμειψα νεῦρα πρώην
καὶ τὴν λύρην ἅπασαν·
κἀγὼ μὲν ᾖδον ἄθλους
Ἡρακλέους· λύρη δὲ
Ἔρωτας ἀντεφώνει.
χαίροιτε λοιπὸν ἡμῖν,
ἥρωες· ἡ λύρη γὰρ
μόνους Ἔρωτας ᾄδει.

Anacreontea

THE PATH TO DEATH

Short the way, but pitiless
The need to walk it.

Guy Davenport (b. 1927)

Λεπτὰ δ' ἀταρπὸς ἀνηλὴς δ' ἀνάγκα.

Alcman, *fragment*

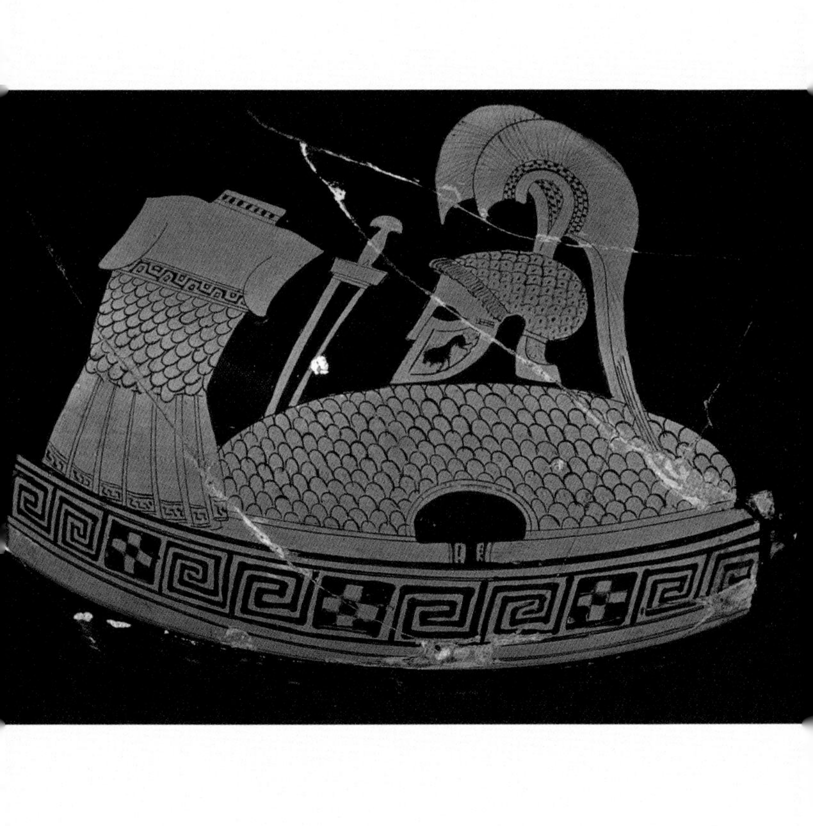

METAMORPHOSIS

I refuse to become a shower of gold,
A bull or a swan as in days of old.
Let Zeus do tricks. Corinna's more willing,
If I remain human and give her a shilling.

Andrew Sinclair (b. 1935)

Οὐ μέλλω ῥεύσειν χρυσός ποτε· βοῦς δὲ γένοιτο
ἄλλος, χὠ μελίθρους κύκνος ἐπηόνιος.
Ζηνὶ φυλασσέσθω τάδε παίγνια· τῇ δὲ Κορίννῃ
τοὺς ὀβολοὺς δώσω τοὺς δύο, κοὐ πέτομαι.

Lollius Bassus, *Greek Anthology V*

LOVE IN HER HAIR

Whether I find thee bright with fair,
Or still as bright with raven hair,
With equal grace thy tresses shine,
Ah, queen, and love will dwell divine
In these thy locks, on that far day
When gold or sable turns to grey.

Andrew Lang (1844–1912)

Εἴτε σε κυανέῃσιν ἀποστίλβουσαν ἐθείραις,
εἴτε πάλιν ξανθαῖς εἶδον, ἄνασσα, κόμαις,
ἴση ἀπ' ἀμφοτέρων λάμπει χάρις. ἦ ῥά γε ταύταις
θριξὶ συνοικήσει καὶ πολιῇσιν Ἔρως.

Anonymous

THE TRUE KNOWLEDGE

Thou knowest all; I seek in vain
What lands to till or sow with seed –
The land is black with brier and weed,
Nor cares for falling tears or rain.

Thou knowest all; I sit and wait
With blinded eyes and hands that fail,
Till the last lifting of the veil
And the first opening of the gate.

Thou knowest all; I cannot see,
I trust I shall not live in vain,
I know that we shall meet again
In some divine eternity.

Oscar Wilde (1854–1900)

Ἀναγκαίως δ' ἔχει
βίον θερίζειν ὥστε κάρπιμον στάχυν,
καὶ τὸν μὲν εἶναι, τὸν δὲ μή.

Euripides, *Hypsipyle, fragment*

ENDURE WHAT LIFE GOD GIVES

Never to have lived is best, ancient writers say:
Never to have drawn the breath of life, never
to have looked into the eye of day;
The second best's a gay goodnight and quickly turn away.

W.B. Yeats (1865–1939)

Μὴ φῦναι τὸν ἅπαντα νι-
κᾷ λόγον· τὸ δ', ἐπεὶ φανῇ,
βῆναι κεῖσ' ὁπόθεν περ ἥ-
κει πολὺ δεύτερον ὡς τάχιστα.

Sophocles, *Oedipus at Colonus*

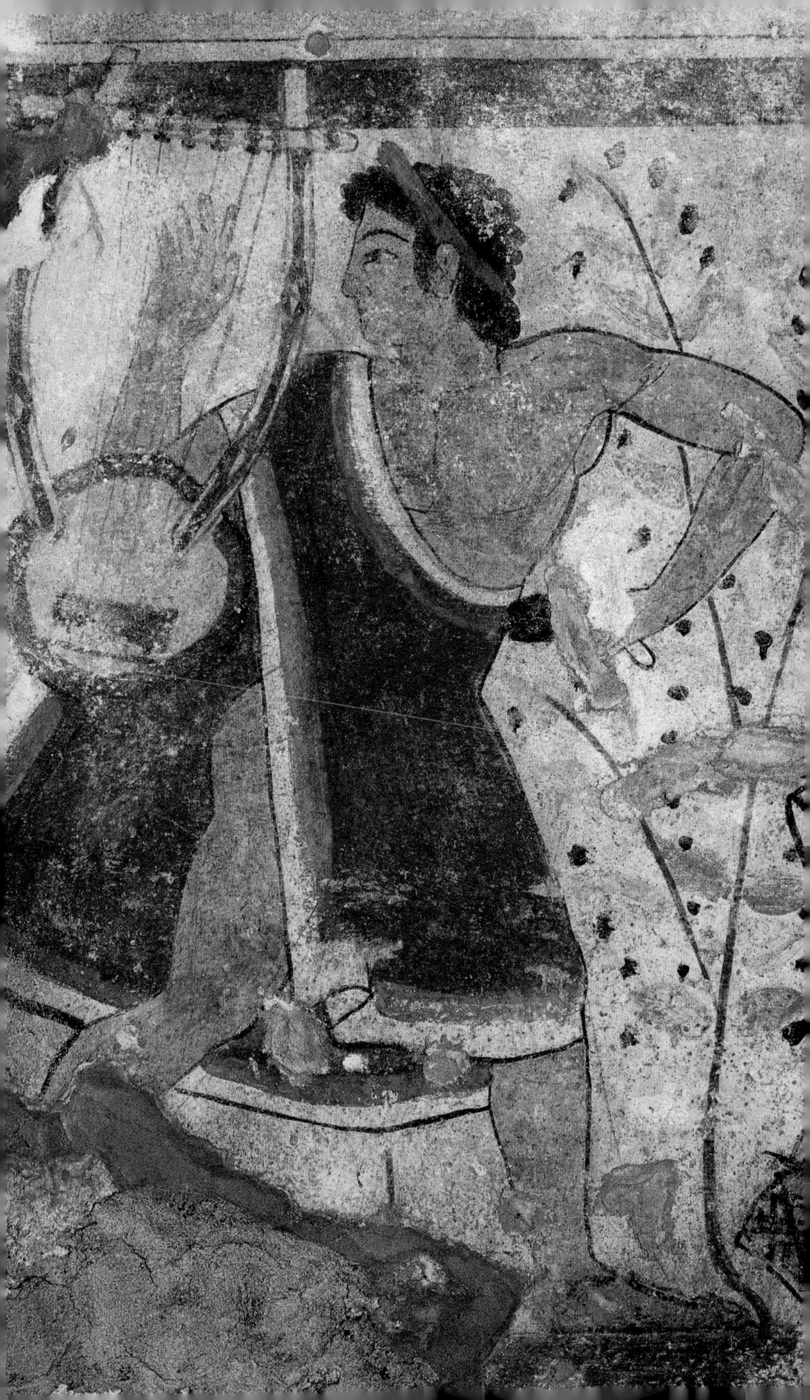

LAND AND SEA

When winds that move not its calm surface sweep
The azure sea, I love the land no more;
The smiles of the serene and tranquil deep
Tempt my unquiet mind. – But when the roar
Of Ocean's gray abyss resounds, and foam
Gathers upon the sea, and vast waves burst,
I turn from the drear aspect to the home
Of Earth and its deep woods, where, interspersed,
When winds blow loud, pines make sweet melody.
Whose house is some lone bark, whose toil the sea,
Whose prey the wandering fish, an evil lot
Has chosen. – But I my languid limbs will fling
Beneath the plane, where the brook's murmuring
Moves the calm spirit, but disturbs it not.

Percy Bysshe Shelley (1792–1822)

Τὰν ἅλα τὰν γλαυκὰν ὅταν ὤνεμος ἀτρέμα βάλλῃ,
τὰν φρένα τὰν δειλὰν ἐρεθίζομαι, οὐδ' ἔτι μοι γᾶ
ἐντὶ φίλα, ποθίει δὲ πολὺ πλέον ἅ με γαλάνα.
ἀλλ' ὅταν ἀχήσῃ πολιὸς βυθός, ἁ δὲ θάλασσα
κυρτὸν ἐπαφρίζῃ, τὰ δὲ κύματα μακρὰ μεμήνῃ,
ἐς χθόνα παπταίνω καὶ δένδρεα, τὰν δ' ἅλα φεύγω,
γᾶ δέ μοι ἀσπαστά, χἀ δάσκιος εὔαδεν ὕλα,
ἔνθα καὶ ἢν πνεύσῃ πολὺς ὤνεμος, ἁ πίτυς ᾄδει.
ἦ κακὸν ὁ γριπεὺς ζώει βίον, ᾧ δόμος ἁ ναῦς,
καὶ πόνος ἐντὶ θάλασσα, καὶ ἰχθύες ἁ πλάνος ἄγρα.
αὐτὰρ ἐμοὶ γλυκὺς ὕπνος ὑπὸ πλατάνῳ βαθυφύλλῳ,
καὶ παγᾶς φιλέοιμι τὸν ἐγγύθεν ἆχον ἀκούειν,
ἃ τέρπει ψοφέοισα τὸν ἀγρικόν, οὐχὶ ταράσσει.

Moschus

CRETAN DANCE

A figured dance succeeds: such once was seen
In lofty Gnossus, for the Cretan queen,
Formed by Daedalean art; a comely band
Of youths and maidens, bounding hand in hand;
The maids in soft cymars of linen dressed;
The youths all graceful in the glossy vest;
Of those the locks with flowery wreaths inrolled;
Of these the sides adorned with swords of gold,
That, glittering gay, from silver belts depend.

Alexander Pope (1688–1744)

Ἐν δὲ χορὸν ποίκιλλε περικλυτὸς ἀμφιγυήεις,
τῷ ἴκελον οἷόν ποτ᾽ ἐνὶ Κνωσῷ εὐρείῃ
Δαίδαλος ἤσκησεν καλλιπλοκάμῳ Ἀριάδνῃ.
ἔνθα μὲν ἠΐθεοι καὶ παρθένοι ἀλφεσίβοιαι
ὠρχεῦντ᾽, ἀλλήλων ἐπὶ καρπῷ χεῖρας ἔχοντες.
τῶν δ᾽ αἱ μὲν λεπτὰς ὀθόνας ἔχον, οἱ δὲ χιτῶνας
εἵατ᾽ ἐϋννήτους, ἦκα στίλβοντας ἐλαίῳ·
καί ῥ᾽ αἱ μὲν καλὰς στεφάνας ἔχον, οἱ δὲ μαχαίρας
εἶχον χρυσείας ἐξ ἀργυρέων τελαμώνων.

Homer, *Iliad XVIII*

MEN AND GODS

Single is the race, single
Of men and of gods;
From a single mother we both draw breath.
But a difference of power in everything
Keeps us apart;
For the one is as nothing, but the brazen sky
Stays a fixed habitation for ever.
Yet we can in greatness of mind
Or of body be like the immortals,
Though we know not to what goal
By day or in the nights
Fate has written that we shall run.

Cecil Maurice Bowra (1898–1971)

Ἓν ἀνδρῶν, ἓν θεῶν γένος· ἐκ μιᾶς δὲ πνέομεν
ματρὸς ἀμφότεροι· διείργει δὲ πᾶσα κεκριμένα
δύναμις, ὡς τὸ μὲν οὐδέν, ὁ δὲ χάλκεος ἀσφαλὲς αἰὲν ἕδος
μένει οὐρανός. ἀλλά τι προσφέρομεν ἔμπαν ἢ μέγαν
νόον ἤτοι φύσιν ἀθανάτοις,
καίπερ ἐφαμερίαν οὐκ εἰδότες οὐδὲ μετὰ νύκτας ἄμμε πότμος
οἵαν τιν' ἔγραψε δραμεῖν ποτὶ στάθμαν.

Pindar, *Nemean Odes VI*

BIOGRAPHICAL NOTES ON THE POETS

ALCMAN (*fl.* 654–611 BC) was a Dorian who lived in Sparta and wrote largely about feasts and festivals. Much of his work consists of choral odes addressed to young girls; he also wrote of birds, horses and food, and with great assurance of night and sleep.

ANACREON of Teos (b. c. 570 BC) was a light-hearted hedonist whose verse reflects a love of the pleasures of drink and sex, usually expressed with elegance and decorum. His delightful and polished lyrics were much imitated in the ancient world, typically in the *Anacreontea*, poems written in his style but probably not composed by him. He died at an advanced age, when a grape pip lodged in his throat.

ARION of Lesbos (*fl.* 628–625 BC) spent much of his time at the court of Periander of Corinth. He is remembered in a legend which tells how, after being thrown overboard while returning to Corinth, he was carried by a dolphin to dry land. In gratitude for this miracle he is said to have composed an ode in praise of Poseidon.

CALLIMACHUS (310–240 BC) was a leading Alexandrian poet who wrote somewhat dry, serious and intellectual long poems, but also moving and passionate epigrams.

EURIPIDES (485–406 BC) nudged drama towards modernism; his characters are unheroic and often appear in domestic situations. He pioneered the idea of a character being in two minds, and reduced the gods to psychological symbols. His understanding of the pathology of extreme human situations involving love, revenge or unfulfilled desire make his plays especially relevant today.

HOMER'S poems were probably composed in the ninth or eighth centuries BC and were admired by all later generations of Greeks. His *Iliad* and *Odyssey* are noted for the nobility, depth and contrast of their characterization, their vivid scene-painting, the dramatic flow of fast-moving narratives, the brilliance of language, and astonishingly true-to-life similes.

LOLLIUS BASSUS (*fl. c.* AD 20) was a native of Smyrna and an epigrammatist, about whom little is known except his name.

Menander of Athens (340–290 BC) was the originator of New Comedy. The plots of his plays – discovered relatives, kidnapped children, plotting slaves, exciting romance, a married man's passion for a prostitute – resemble soap-opera to the modern reader.

Mnasalcas (*fl. c.* 250 BC) came from Sicyon, west of Corinth. Some of his verses were admired in antiquity for being 'needle sharp'.

Moschus (*fl. c.*150 BC) came from Syracuse and was a playful and hedonistic poet who re-worked the old myths in a graceful and bucolic manner.

Palladas (*c.* AD 360–430), an Alexandrian epigrammatist, wrote in a tone of gloomy nihilism against Christian monasticism, which had become very fashionable in his lifetime, inveighing against it with as much bleak austerity as the monks were alleged to practise.

Perses of Thebes (*fl. c.* 320 BC) fashioned verses that were used as tomb inscriptions rather than being mere stylish literary exercises.

Pindar (518–438 BC) lived into the age of democratic accountability, but he remained an old-fashioned aristocrat to the last, believing that human excellence

derived either from proper breeding or from divine origin. His magnificent lyric odes were renowned throughout antiquity.

SAPPHO of Lesbos (*fl. c.* 600 BC) was considered the greatest lyric poet of the ancient world, referred to by Plato as 'the tenth muse'. She wrote incomparably of the power of Eros to release the forces of the spirit and to unite sensuous loving individuals in a graceful and playful dance. No other poet has matched her passion and tenderness, nor her capacity to encompass the simultaneous exaltation and tragedy of love.

SOPHOCLES (496–406 BC) was renowned for the humanity of his plays. His dramas located tragedy in human individuality, and he drew from the pain a powerful lyricism. He mistrusted human reason, believing that the higher laws of the gods were the laws of the universe; at the same time, he infused his characters with a profound dignity, even at the moment of their downfall.

THEOGNIS of Megara (*fl. c.* 550–540 BC) composed a number of elegiac verses concerned with the moral development of his friend Cyrnus, for whom he expressed a strong, if rather withdrawn passionate devotion, but by whom he was frequently let down.

A NOTE ON GREEK PAINTING

Archaeology has shown us that painting in the Greek world goes back at least 3,500 years. During the Late Bronze Age cultures on Crete and the Cyclades Islands, the walls of both public and private buildings were often covered with elaborate frescoes. Excavations at Acroteri on the island of Thera (Santorini) have brought to light whole rooms with painted walls miraculously preserved when debris from a violent volcanic eruption covered the site in around 1500 BC (see pages 9, 14, 26–7). Excavations on nearby Crete, particularly at Knossos, have also revealed fragments of paintings on palace walls (45, 48–9, 58, 65, 66–7).

When much of Greece emerged from its 'Dark Age' – a period of dire poverty following the decline of the Bronze Age civilizations – painting seems to have been limited at first to the surfaces of ceramic vessels. However, by the seventh century BC there is evidence of the development of large-scale painting on walls and wooden panels. Unfortunately, none of these thousands of monumental paintings has survived, though we know about them from the descriptions of several ancient authors, particularly Pausanias, a

second-century AD traveller who wrote a guide book to Greece describing many paintings in great detail. Beyond that we can get some sense of the lost paintings through their reflections in other art forms.

Over 50,000 Athenian vases decorated with figures have come down to us. The pictures painted on them are usually scenes from daily life or mythological stories. Most of the vases are painted in one of three techniques. The earliest technique (pre-600 BC) is known as black-figure: figures are painted in black against the natural reddish background of Attic clay, and details are incised or added with white or red paint (10, 18, 47). Around 530 BC a new technique called red-figure was introduced, which is the opposite of black-figure. The figures are reserved – that is, they are left in the reddish colour of the clay, while the background is painted black (21, 36, 41, 42, 51, 55, 57, 69). In a third technique, called white-ground, the surface of the vase is covered with a white slip. The figures are then drawn in outline, and pastel washes are sometimes used to highlight details (5, 35).

During the last quarter of the fifth century BC, some Attic painters moved to Greek colonies in South Italy where they began to produce red-figure vases using local clay. Within a generation or so local painters developed their own styles, which tended to be more elaborate and often more colourful than the original

Attic models. In South Italy this tradition continued down into the early third century BC (23, 24, 29, 76).

The Etruscans, who inhabited the area of Italy between the Tiber and Arno rivers, were a prime market for Attic black- and red-figure vases. Thousands of Attic vases have been found in their rich tombs, and some of the tombs themselves, particularly at Tarquinia and Vulci, have walls painted with lively scenes of dancing and dining that to one degree or another reflect aspects of Greek painting (17, 39, 63). Though the Greeks rarely painted their tombs, one remarkable exception is the early fifth-century BC Tomb of the Diver found at Paestum (the Greek colony of Poseidonia). The four rectangular slabs forming the tomb are painted with a continuous banquet scene, while the cover slab shows a youth diving into the sea (12–13, 52–3). Even after 2,500 years, images such as these continue to captivate us with their realistic and beautiful depictions of the human form.

Thomas H. Carpenter

Charles J. Ping Professor of Humanities and Professor of Classics
Ohio University

ACKNOWLEDGMENTS

The Publishers would like to thank the following for permission to use copyright material: Cambridge University Press for twelve lines of Sophocles' *Antigone* from *Poems* (1935) by F.L. Lucas; Faber & Faber Ltd for three lines from Sophocles' *Oedipus Rex: An English Version* (1951) by Dudley Fitts and Robert Fitzgerald; Harcourt for the excerpt from 'Oedipus Rex' in *Sophocles, The Oedipus Cycle: an English Version* by Dudly Fitts and Robert Fitzgerald, copyright 1949 by Harcourt, Inc. and renewed 1977 by Cornelia Fitts and Robert Fitzgerald, reprinted by permission of the publisher; Oxford University Press for extracts from *The Oxford Book of Greek Verse in Translation* (1938) edited by T.F. Higham and C.M. Bowra and for eleven lines of Sophocles from *The Greek Genius and Its Meaning to Us* (2nd edn, 1917) by R.W. Livingstone; Penguin Books Ltd for thirteen lines from *The Odes of Pindar* translated by C.M. Bowra (Penguin Classics, 1969) copyright © The Estate of C.M. Bowra, 1969; the Regents of the University of California and the University of California Press for three fragments from *Sappho: A New Translation* (1958) by Mary Barnard; A.P. Watt Ltd, on behalf of Michael B. Yeats, and Charles Scribner & Sons for four lines of Sophocles' *Oedipus at Colonus* from *The Collected Poems of W.B. Yeats* (1950); and Weidenfeld & Nicolson for four lines by Lollius Bassus translated by Andrew Sinclair in *Selections from the Greek Anthology*. The Publishers have made every effort to contact all copyright holders and would like to hear from any that they were unable to trace.

PHOTOGRAPHIC ACKNOWLEDGMENTS

For permission to reproduce the frescoes, mosaics and vase paintings on the following pages and for supplying photographs, the Publishers would like to thank: **AKG London** 47; **AKG London/John Hios** 14; **AKG London/Erich Lessing** 9, 41, 42, 45, 52–3, 55, 57, 58, 69; **Ashmolean Museum, Oxford** 21 (1886.587); © **Copyright The British Museum** 60; **The J. Paul Getty Museum** 10 (79.AE.147), 30–1 (85.AA.107), 36 (84.AE.569), 51 (91.AE.10); **Ministry of Culture, Athens** 5, 33, 35, 48–9, 65, 66–7; **Museo Eoliano di Lipari** 23, 24, 29, 76; **Scala, Florence** 12–13, 17, 18, 39, 63; **Thera Foundation, Piraeus** endpapers, 26–7 (Ch. Doumas, *The Wall Paintings of Thera*, Idryma Theras – Petros M. Nomikos, Athens, 1992)

First published in Great Britain in 2000 by Frances Lincoln Limited,
4 Torriano Mews, Torriano Avenue, London NW5 2RZ

British Library Cataloguing in Publication Data available on request
ISBN 978-0-7112-1316-6
IMAGES AND VERSE SELECTED BY YVONNE WHITEMAN
Biographical notes on the poets and ancient Greek poetry sourcing by Christopher Walker

Set in Tiepolo; ancient Greek set in Porson 2000 by Regent Typesetting, London
Printed and bound by Kwong Fat Offset Printing Co Ltd, Hong Kong
3 5 7 9 8 6 4